When I Grow Up

Jan Burchett & Sara Vogler
Illustrated by Carol Thompson

When I grow up, I want to be a vet.

Oops!

Maybe I won't be a vet.

What else can I be?

When I grow up, I want to be
a hairdresser.

Oops!

Maybe I won’t be a hairdresser.

What else can I be?

When I grow up, I want to be a firefighter.

Oops!

Maybe I won't be a firefighter.

What else can I be?

When I grow up, I want to be a gardener.

Oops!
Maybe I won't be a gardener.
What else can I be?

When I grow up, I want to be a builder.

Oops!
Maybe I won’t be a builder.

Maybe I won’t grow up just yet!